INSECTS

DAVID BURNIE

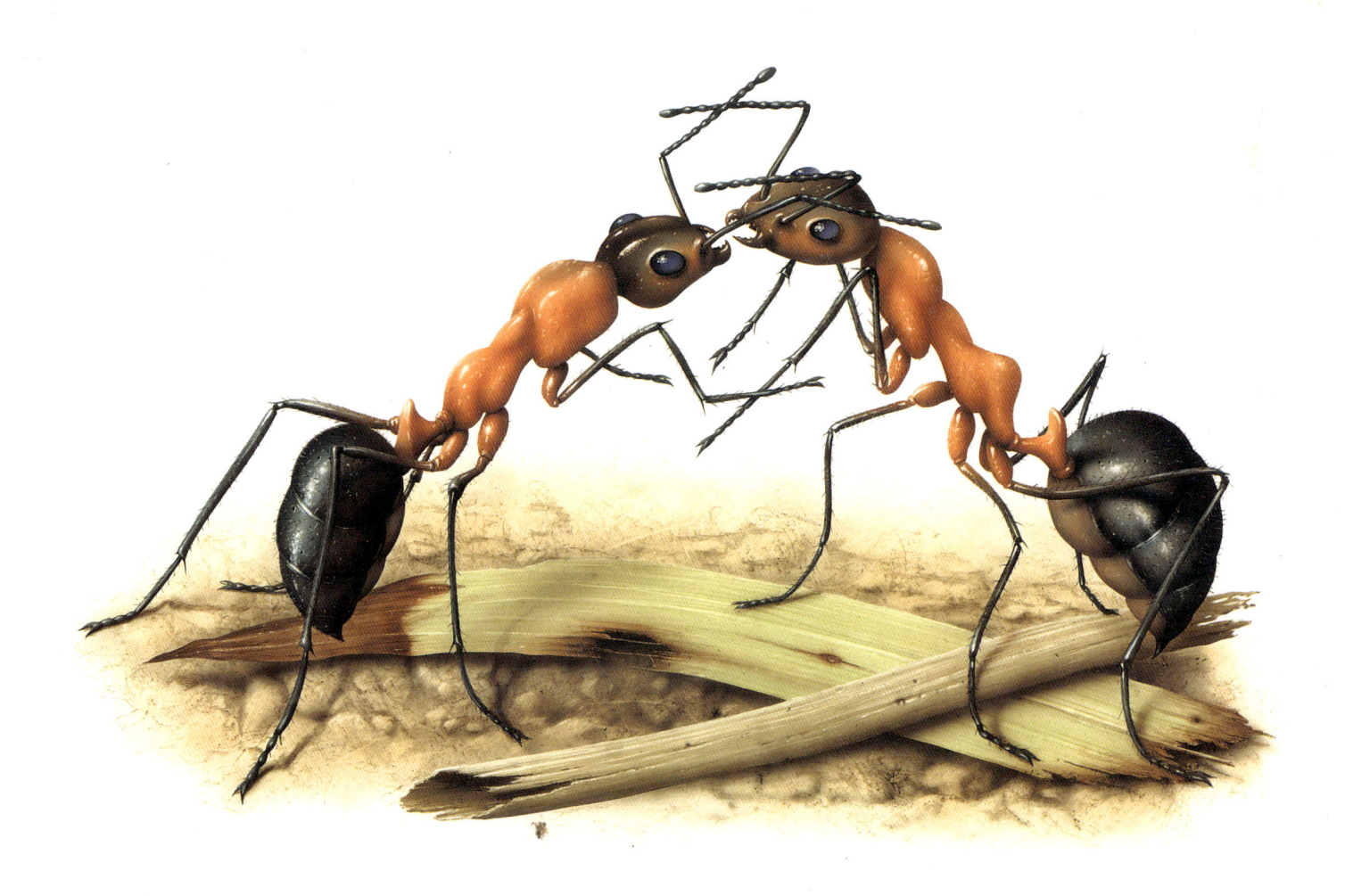

HAMLYN

ACKNOWLEDGEMENTS

The publisher would like to thank the following individuals and organizations
for providing the photographs used in this book:

Ardea / MW Gillam: 31 centre left.

Bruce Coleman Ltd / Jane Burton: 22 top right, / M P L Fogden: 27 below right, / Jeff Foott Productions: 34 top right, / Michael Freeman: 42 top right, / Peter A Hinchliffe: 19 below right, / Dr Frieder Sauer: 37 below right, 43 top left, / Kim Taylor: 10 below right, 20 top right, 21 top right, 28 centre left, 45 below left, / Gunter Ziesler: 34 below left.

Steve Gschmeisner: 16 top right.

Hutchison Library / Nancy Durrell McKenna: 45 centre left. Frank Lane Picture Agency / T Davidson: 26 top right.

Microscopix Photo Library / Andrew Syred: 7 top left, 14 15, 45 top left. The Natural History Museum, London: 17 top left.

Natural Science Photos / Richard Revels: 25 top right.

NHPA / Anthony Bannister: 15 below left, 25 top left, 27 below left, / Laurie Campbell: 43 below left, / James Carmichael: 38 below right, / Stephen Dalton: 38 below left, 43 below right, / Ron Fotheringham: 37 top left, / George Gainsburgh: 39 left, / Daniel Heuclin: 35 centre right.

Oxford Scientific Films: 27 below centre, / G I Bernard: 23 top right, / Alastair Shay: 4 /5.

Premaphotos Wildlife / K G Preston-Mafham: 21 top left, 37 top right, 44 top right.

Science Photo Library: 17 below right, / George Bernard: 35 top right, / Dr Tony Brain & David Parker: 47 below right, / Jean-Loup Carmet: 45 below right, / CNRI: 36 below right, / Judy Davidson: 7 below right, / Manfred Kage: 16 below left, / Claude Nuridsany & Marie Perennou: 7 below left, / David Scharf: 15 below right.

ILLUSTRATORS:

Mike Atkinson (Garden Studio): 12 top right, 13 top right, 22-23 main, 24-25 main, 36, 37 bottom, 45 top right.

John Butler (Ian Flemming & Associates): 12-13 bottom.

Wayne Ford (Wildlife Art Agency): 26-27, 46-47 insets.

Alan Male: 8-9, 16-17, 32-33, 40-41.

The Maltings Partnership: 13 bottom right, 14, 18-19 top, 31 right, 34-35 main, 44 bottom insets, 46-47 main.

Brian McIntyre (Ian Flemming & Associates): title page, 11, 18 main, 19 top right and bottom left, 30-31 main.

Roger Goringe (Garden Studio): 4, 5, 11 bottom, 15 top, 30 inset, 31 top, 43 top and bottom.

Andrew Robinson (Garden Studio): 10, 20, 21, 28-29.

Mark Stewart (Wildlife Art Agency): 6 main, 34-35 inset and bottom.

Ed Stuart: 6 inset, 7 centre, 42 bottom left, 44 main.

George Thompson: 39 top right, 42 bottom right.

David Wright (Kathy Jakeman Illustration): 38 top right, 39 bottom left.

HAMLYN CHILDREN'S BOOKS:

Editor: Veronica Pennycook
Designer: Nick Avery
Production Controller: Mark Leonard
Picture Researcher: Anna Smith

First published in Great Britain 1995
by Hamlyn Children's Books,
an imprint of Reed Children's Books,
Michelin House, 81 Fulham Road, London SW3 6RB,
and Auckland, Melbourne, Singapore and Toronto.

Copyright © 1995 Reed International Books Limited

All rights reserved. No part of this publication may be reproduced,
stored in a retrieval system, or transmitted, in any form or by any means,
electronic, mechanical, photocopying, recording, or otherwise, without the
prior permission of the copyright holders.

ISBN 0 600 58395 3

A CIP catalogue record for this book is available at the British Library.
Books printed and bound by Proost, Belgium.

CONTENTS

INSECTS **4**

LIFE IN A CASE **6**

INSIDE INSECTS 8

HOW INSECTS BREATHE **10**

FLIGHT **12**

SENSING THE WORLD **14**

FEEDING AND DIGESTION 16

KEEPING IN TOUCH **18**

HOW INSECTS REPRODUCE **20**

CHANGING SHAPE **22**

CYCLES OF LIFE **24**

INSECTS AND PLANTS **26**

INSECTS UNDERWATER **28**

LIVING TOGETHER **30**

INSECT ARCHITECTS 32

INCREDIBLE JOURNEYS **34**

PARASITIC INSECTS **36**

ATTACK AND DEFENCE **38**

CAMOUFLAGE AND MIMICRY 40

INSECT COLOURS **42**

DANGEROUS INSECTS **44**

INSECTS INDOORS **46**

INDEX **48**

INSECTS

Insects are one of nature's greatest success stories. They live almost everywhere except in the sea, and they eat an amazing variety of food, including blood, leaves, pollen, wool, and even crude oil. Many people do not like insects because some of them sting or bite, and because some spread diseases. But as you'll find out in this book, insects are fascinating animals, and most do no harm.

WHAT IS AN INSECT?

An insect is an animal that has a hard body case. The case is made up by small plates, and joints between the plates allow the insect to move. The case protects the insect's internal organs, and also stops the insect drying out.

An insect's body is divided into three parts. The front part, or head, carries the insect's mouthparts, and many of its sense organs. The middle part, or thorax, usually carries three pairs of legs. In most insects, it also carries one or two pairs of wings. The rear part, or abdomen, contains part of the insect's digestive system, and its reproductive organs.

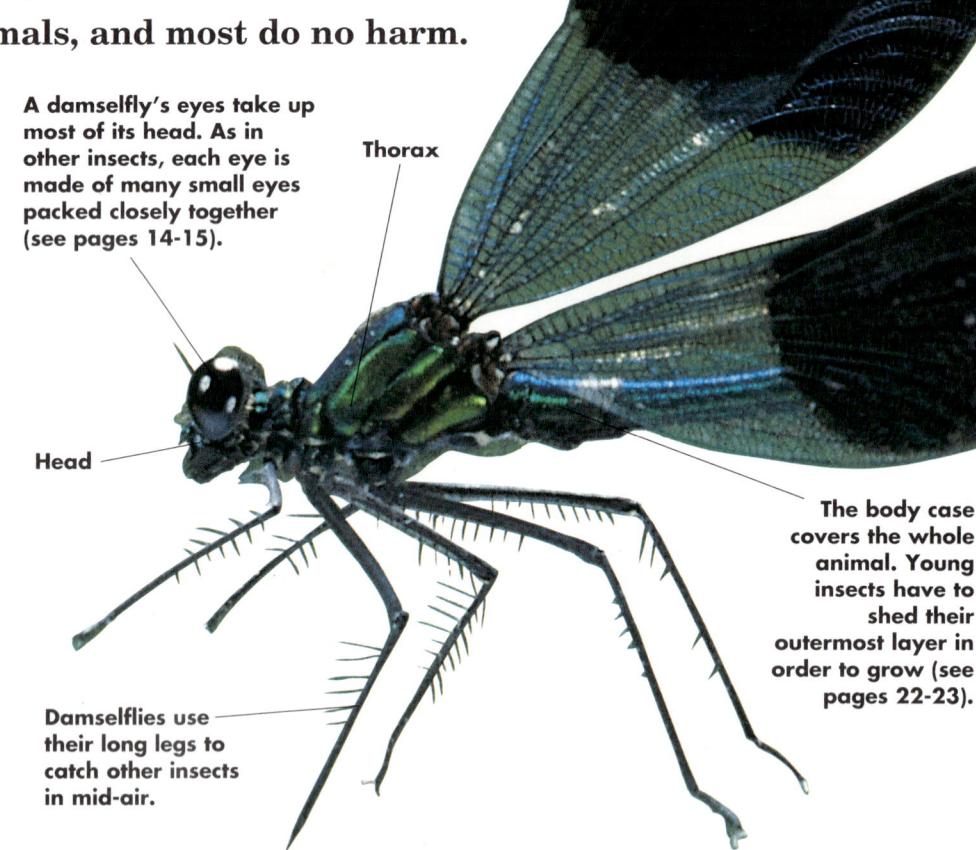

A damselfly's eyes take up most of its head. As in other insects, each eye is made of many small eyes packed closely together (see pages 14-15).

Thorax

Head

Damselflies use their long legs to catch other insects in mid-air.

The body case covers the whole animal. Young insects have to shed their outermost layer in order to grow (see pages 22-23).

INSECT LOOK-ALIKES

Insects are not the only animals that have bodies with a jointed case. The animals shown here are often mistaken for insects, but they all belong to different groups in the animal world.
Woodlice actually belong to the crustacean group, spiders to the arachnid group, and centipedes to the chilopod group.

Crustaceans have jointed bodies and legs, but they never have wings. Most live in the sea, although the woodlouse lives on land.

Centipedes have a long flattened body with many pairs of jointed legs. They have two poison claws near their head.

Spiders have four pairs of jointed legs, not three. Unlike insects, their bodies are divided into two parts, and they do not have compound eyes.

INSECT FAMILIES

Scientists divide insects into about 30 different groups, called families. The insects in each family share important features, such as scaly wings or chewing mouthparts, and they grow up in a similar way (see pages 22-23). Some insect families contain less than a hundred different species, but other families have tens or hundreds of thousands of different species. Insects from some of the most important families are shown here.

Damselflies have two similar pairs of wings. In some insects, the forewings and hindwings are very different (see pages 12-13).

An insect's body is made up of units called segments. In the abdomen, the segments are easy to see.

Beetle family
Insects with rounded bodies and hard wing-cases. About 380,000 species.

Dragonfly family
Insects with long bodies and two pairs of stiff wings. About 5,000 species.

Springtail family
Primitive wingless insects with a springing tail. About 15,000 species.

Fly family
Insects with a single pair of wings. About 65,000 species.

Grasshopper family
Insects with long bodies, leathery forewings and powerful hindlegs. About 20,000 species.

Bee and wasp family
Insects with forewings and hindwings that hook together. About 100,000 species.

Butterfly and moth family
Insects with wings that are covered with scales. About 140,000 species.

Bug family
Insects with piercing or sucking mouthparts. About 60,000 species.

So far, about 1 million kinds of insect have been identified and named by scientists, and about 10,000 new ones are discovered each year. Some scientists think that the real number of insect species on Earth may be as high as 10 million. Insects are so varied that we will never know exactly how many kinds there are.

LIFE IN A CASE

Your skeleton is inside your body. It keeps your body in shape, and provides a framework that your muscles can pull against. An insect's body is arranged the other way around. Its skeleton is on the outside, and its muscles and other body parts are hidden away inside. This kind of skeleton is often called a body case. Unlike a bony skeleton, it cannot get bigger once it has formed.

ARMOUR PLATING

A beetle's body case is made of a substance rather like plastic. It is strong and waterproof, and also quite light. The case has many plates, and these meet at flexible joints which allow the beetle to move. The case covers the beetle's entire body, including its legs and head, and even its eyes.

Not all insects have body cases that are as tough as a beetle's. Insects which are not yet adult, such as caterpillars and grubs, have paper-thin cases, so their bodies feel soft.

TUBES ON THE MOVE

An insect's leg is like a chain of hard tubes. The tubes meet at flexible joints, and muscles inside the tubes make the leg move. Insects have legs of many different shapes, but they are all built on the same plan.

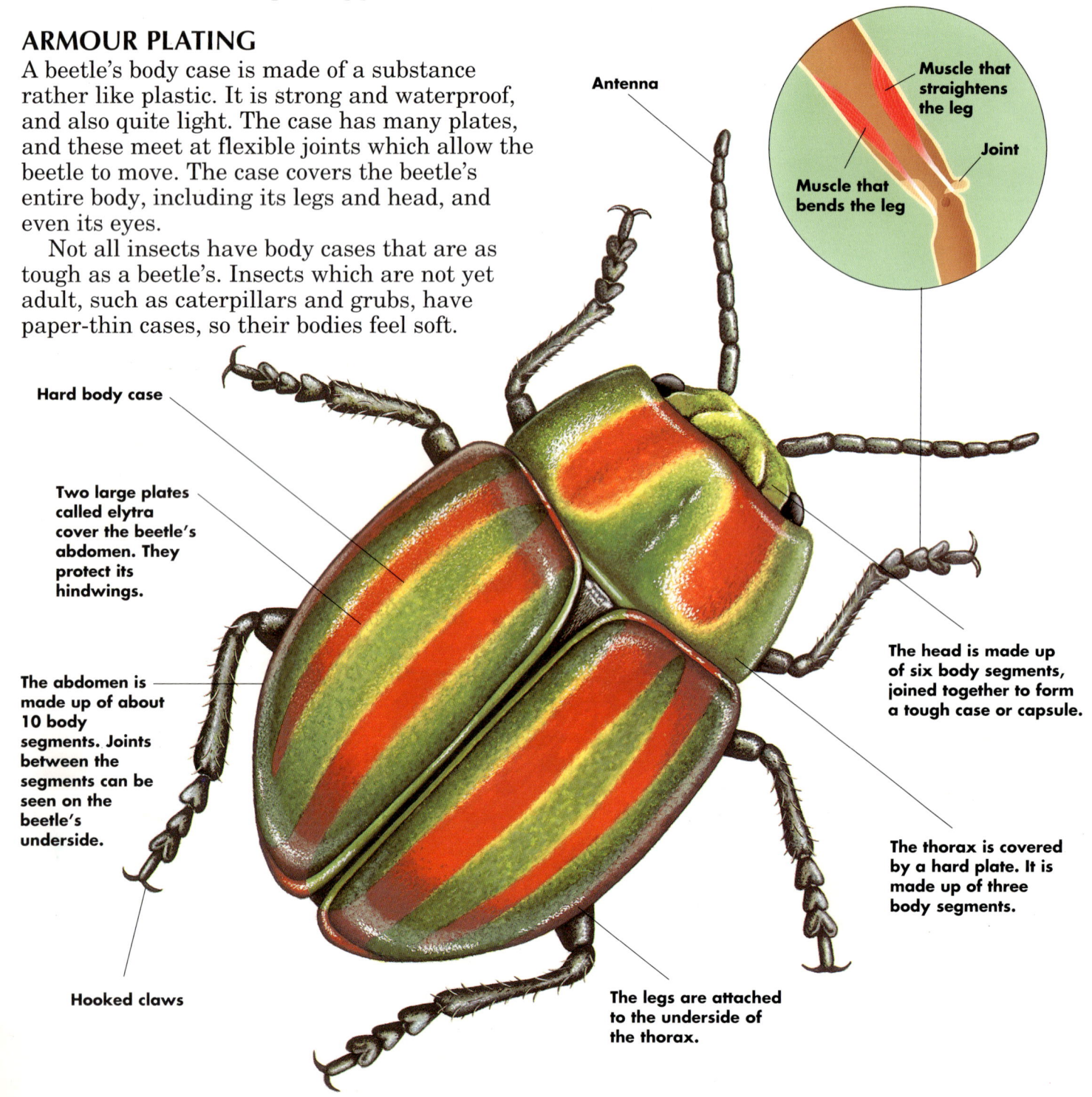

Muscle that straightens the leg

Joint

Muscle that bends the leg

Antenna

Hard body case

Two large plates called elytra cover the beetle's abdomen. They protect its hindwings.

The abdomen is made up of about 10 body segments. Joints between the segments can be seen on the beetle's underside.

Hooked claws

The head is made up of six body segments, joined together to form a tough case or capsule.

The thorax is covered by a hard plate. It is made up of three body segments.

The legs are attached to the underside of the thorax.

INSECTS

6

SOMETHING ON THE SURFACE

When seen under a microscope, an insect's body surface looks like a strange landscape. Its hard body plates carry tiny structures that play a vital part in its daily struggle to survive.

DID YOU KNOW?

◆ The world's heaviest insect is the goliath beetle from central Africa. It is up to 15 cm long and weighs up to 100 grams.

◆ Body cases are light only if they are small. If insects were as big as humans, they would be so heavy that they could not move.

◆ Although it is only 5 cm long, the atlas moth has a wingspan of up to 30 cm.

Honeybees have tiny glands that ooze wax on to the underside of their bodies. They scrape off the wax, and use it to make honeycombs.

Many insects have special hairs that detect air currents or vibrations. These warn the insect when something is approaching.

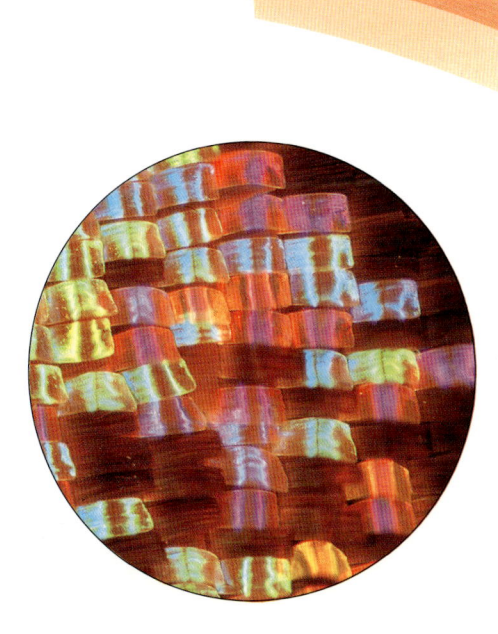

Butterflies and moths have microscopic scales that cover most of their bodies. On the wings, the scales overlap like tiles on a roof. This photograph shows the wing of a brilliantly-coloured Urania moth, from Madagascar.

As an insect grows up, it sheds its skin, or moults, several times. This photograph shows an adult cicada emerging from its larval skin. At first, the adult's new skin is soft, which makes it vulnerable to attack from its enemies. The skin soon hardens.

INSIDE INSECTS

Each insect is built on the same basic plan, with many different internal organs that work together in groups, called body systems. On these pages, we've used a grasshopper to reveal four body systems important to all insects.

MUSCULAR SYSTEM

The picture to the right reveals a grasshopper's muscular system. The muscles contract, or become shorter, to make part of the body move. An adult grasshopper has nearly 1,000 different muscles. Its muscles can pull, but they cannot push, so most of them are arranged in groups that work in opposite directions.

CIRCULATORY SYSTEM

The circulatory system carries blood around the body. The blood delivers food substances to all the cells, and defends the body from bacteria.

A grasshopper's circulatory system is shown in the picture on the far right. Like all insects, the grasshopper has several hearts, and these are set in a row. The blood is pumped forwards along a tube, but it travels back through open spaces in the body.

MUSCULAR SYSTEM (right)

Muscles that...
1 ...move antennae
2 ...close jaws
3 ...lift base of front legs
4 ...lift base of middle legs
5 ...pull wings up and down
6 ...are used in jumping
7 ...shorten abdomen

CIRCULATORY SYSTEM
(far right)

1 Main blood vessel
2 Hearts
3 Blood entering main blood vessel
4 Blood leaving main blood vessel
5 Blood returning through spaces in body

REPRODUCTIVE SYSTEM

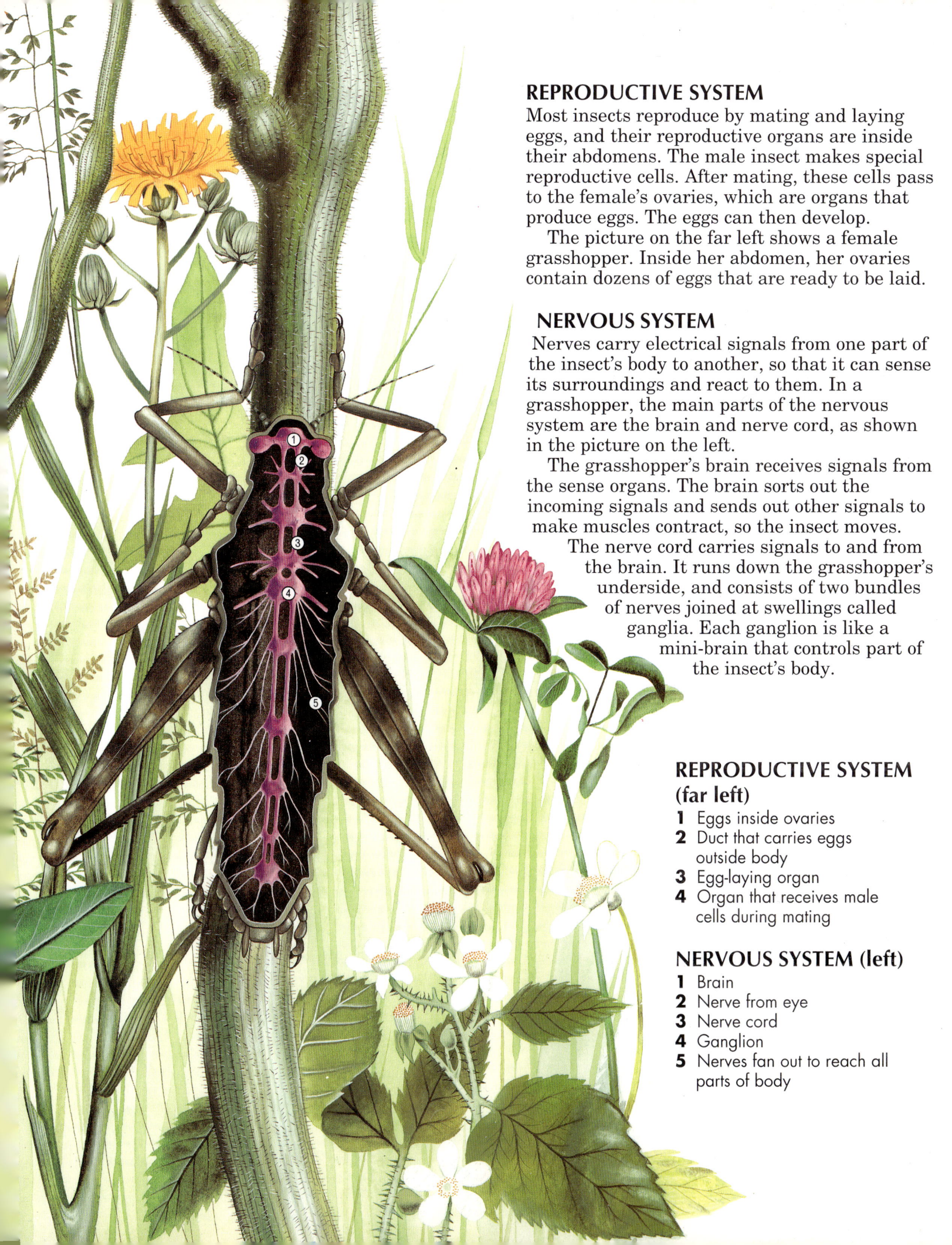

Most insects reproduce by mating and laying eggs, and their reproductive organs are inside their abdomens. The male insect makes special reproductive cells. After mating, these cells pass to the female's ovaries, which are organs that produce eggs. The eggs can then develop.

The picture on the far left shows a female grasshopper. Inside her abdomen, her ovaries contain dozens of eggs that are ready to be laid.

NERVOUS SYSTEM

Nerves carry electrical signals from one part of the insect's body to another, so that it can sense its surroundings and react to them. In a grasshopper, the main parts of the nervous system are the brain and nerve cord, as shown in the picture on the left.

The grasshopper's brain receives signals from the sense organs. The brain sorts out the incoming signals and sends out other signals to make muscles contract, so the insect moves.

The nerve cord carries signals to and from the brain. It runs down the grasshopper's underside, and consists of two bundles of nerves joined at swellings called ganglia. Each ganglion is like a mini-brain that controls part of the insect's body.

REPRODUCTIVE SYSTEM (far left)
1. Eggs inside ovaries
2. Duct that carries eggs outside body
3. Egg-laying organ
4. Organ that receives male cells during mating

NERVOUS SYSTEM (left)
1. Brain
2. Nerve from eye
3. Nerve cord
4. Ganglion
5. Nerves fan out to reach all parts of body

INSIDE INSECTS

HOW INSECTS BREATHE

All animals need oxygen to survive. When you breathe in, oxygen travels through your lungs and into your blood, and the blood then carries the oxygen around your body. But insects do not have lungs, and their blood is not much good at carrying oxygen. Instead, they breathe with a system of tiny air-pipes, called tracheae. These pipes reach inside an insect's body.

An insect's air-tubes are always open so that air can flow. The ends of the air-tubes are 100 times thinner than a human hair.

Spiracle
Main tracheae

TWO-WAY TRAFFIC

A flea has a row of small openings down each side of its body. These openings are called spiracles, and they are entrances to air-pipes inside the insect. Oxygen flows through the spiracles and into the air-pipes, and as it goes deeper and deeper into the body, the pipes get narrower and narrower. Eventually, the oxygen leaves the pipes and enters the body's cells. At the same time, a waste gas called carbon dioxide travels in the opposite direction. It flows out of the cells and into the air-pipes, and then through the spiracles to the air outside.

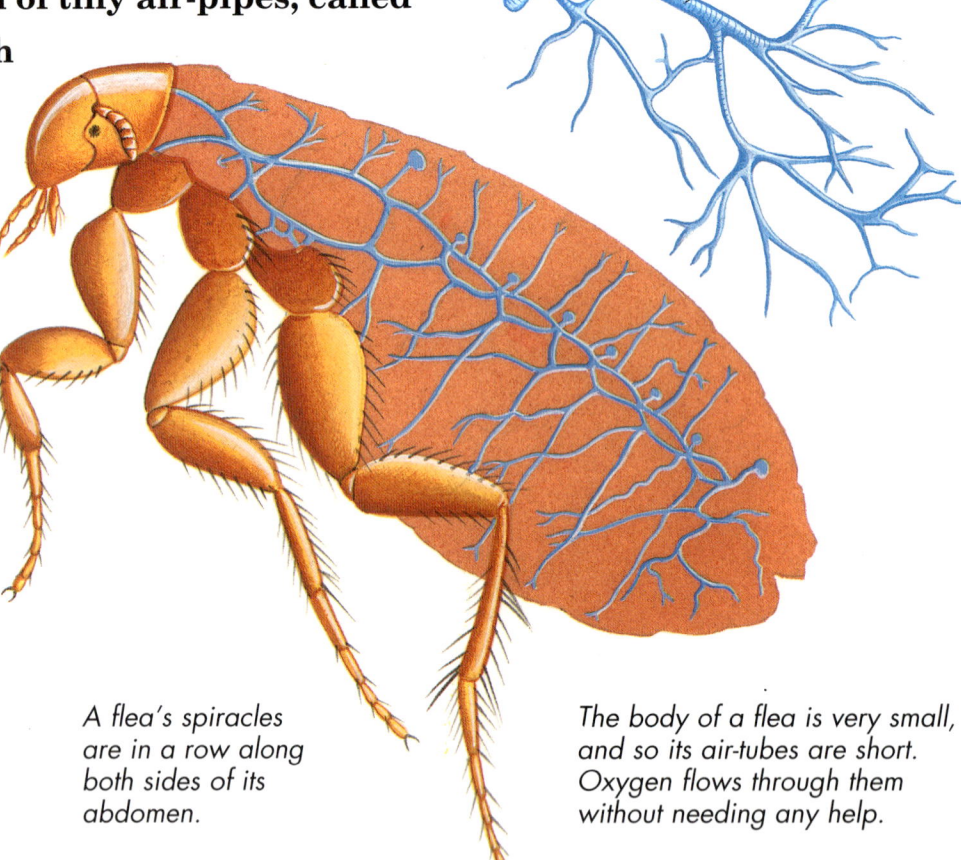

A flea's spiracles are in a row along both sides of its abdomen.

The body of a flea is very small, and so its air-tubes are short. Oxygen flows through them without needing any help.

TAKING A BREATH

Small insects do not have to take breaths because oxygen can easily flow to all parts of their bodies. Large insects, such as grasshoppers and crickets, need more oxygen, and so they often pump it through their bodies. A cricket's air-tubes are connected to chambers called air sacs. The cricket squeezes the sacs to pump air out of its body. When it stops squeezing, the sacs return to their normal shape, and a fresh supply of air is sucked in.

A great green bushcricket has a large body, and its muscles help oxygen move through its air-tubes. This photo shows a row of spiracles along the middle of its abdomen.

OPEN AND SHUT

An insect's spiracles are like tiny portholes. When the insect is active, they open wide so that as much oxygen as possible can enter the body. When the insect is resting, its spiracles become narrower, and sometimes close altogether. By closing its spiracles, the insect prevents water vapour escaping from its body. This stops it from drying out.

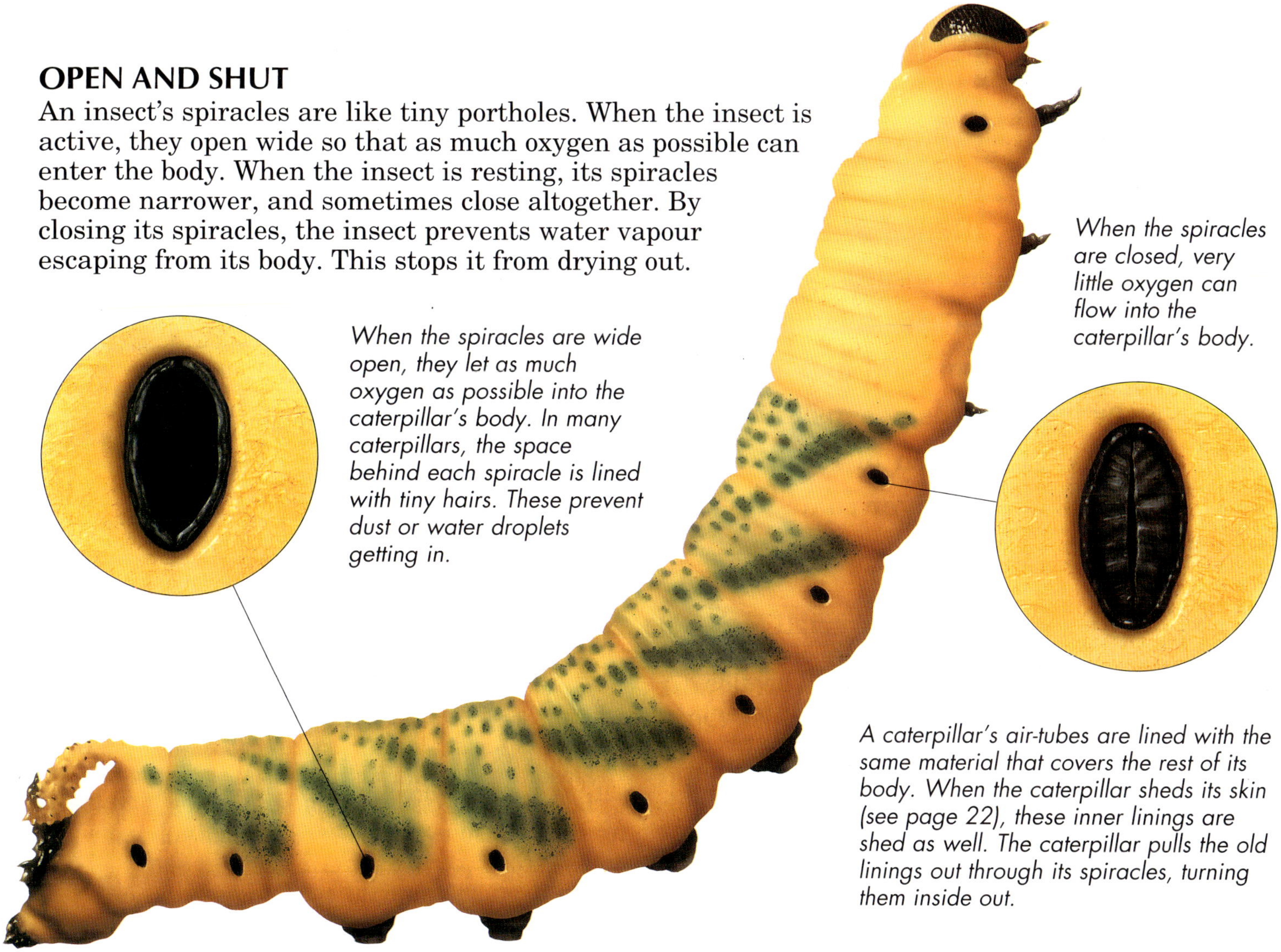

When the spiracles are wide open, they let as much oxygen as possible into the caterpillar's body. In many caterpillars, the space behind each spiracle is lined with tiny hairs. These prevent dust or water droplets getting in.

When the spiracles are closed, very little oxygen can flow into the caterpillar's body.

A caterpillar's air-tubes are lined with the same material that covers the rest of its body. When the caterpillar sheds its skin (see page 22), these inner linings are shed as well. The caterpillar pulls the old linings out through its spiracles, turning them inside out.

BREATHING UNDERWATER

Many insects spend part or all of their lives in water. Some of these insects collect oxygen from the air, using special tubes that break through the water's surface. Others collect oxygen from the water itself, like fish.

These insects still have a system of air-pipes but they do not have spiracles. Oxygen flows into their air-pipes through organs called gills. You can read more about underwater insects on pages 28-29.

The backswimmer traps a bubble of air around its body, and then dives. It has to swim hard to stop floating back up.

The rat-tailed maggot lives in stagnant water, where there is little oxygen. It breathes through a special pipe.

This mosquito larva breathes through a small tube. A ring of water-repellent hairs stops water flowing in.

A mayfly larva has gills. Oxygen from the water passes through the thin surface of the gills and into the air-pipes.

SENSING THE WORLD

For all insects, life is a dangerous business. Insects have to get food and reproduce, but they also have to avoid being attacked and eaten. To find the information they need to survive, insects use their senses.

DID YOU KNOW?
- We cannot see ultra-violet light, but honeybees can. Many flowers have special ultraviolet patterns which guide honeybees to their food.
- A red admiral butterfly is 200 times better at sensing sugar than a human
- Some male moths can smell the scent of a female moth when she is over 3 km away.

ON THE ALERT
A hornet has keen senses, and is quick to spot the chance of a meal. Most of its sense organs are in its head. It has two large compound eyes, and also three much smaller eyes, called ocelli, arranged in a triangle. The hornet's compound eyes provide a picture of the world around it, and are particularly good at sensing anything that moves. The ocelli probably tell it how bright or dark its surroundings are. The hornet uses its antennae to touch, to smell, and to taste food. Bristles around its head detect currents in the air, and warn it if anything moves nearby.

HOW COMPOUND EYES WORK
A compound eye contains many tiny eyes packed together. Each 'eyelet' focuses light with two lenses, and it senses just a small part of the scene outside. The insect's brain gathers the signals from the eyelets, and uses them to put together a picture of the surroundings.

It is impossible to tell exactly what an insect sees, but scientists know that insects can detect some colours that are invisible to us. How clearly an insect sees depends on the number of eyelets in its eyes. Some ants have just a few eyelets, but dragonflies can have over 25,000.

Sensory bristles

Large compound eye

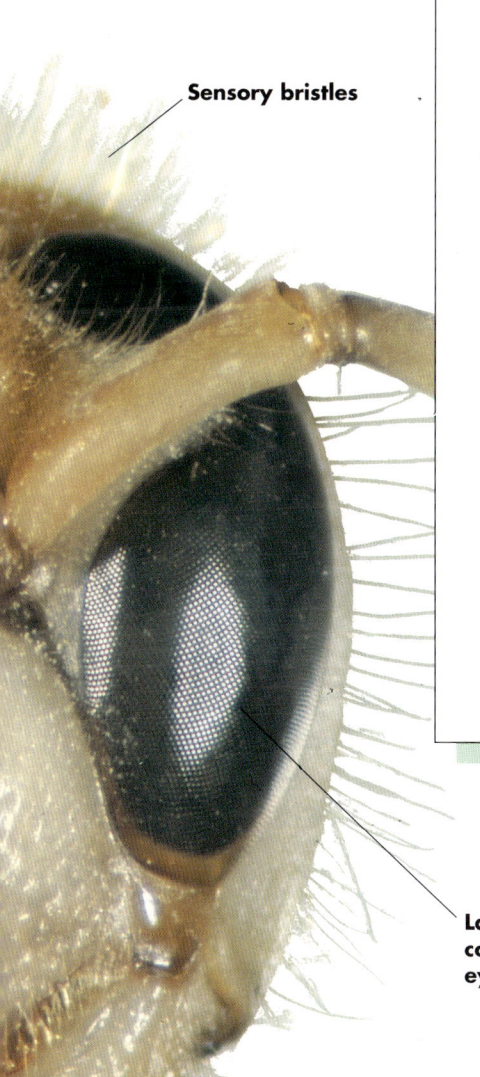

ANTENNAE

An insect's antennae are much more than 'feelers'. Insects use their antennae to touch, to taste things, to smell the air, and sometimes even to hear. The shape of antennae varies between different kinds of insect, and also sometimes between males and females in the same species.

Butterflies have slender antennae with club-shaped tips.

A weevil's antennae are on its long snout. They have a sharp bend, or 'elbow'.

A bush cricket's antennae are always on the move as it searches for food.

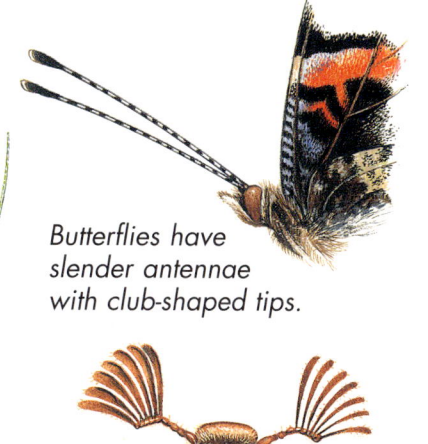

A male cockchafer's antennae open like fans. They help it find a mate.

HOW MANY SENSES?

Like humans, insects have many different senses. They see, hear, taste, smell and touch, but they also have senses that tell them which way up they are, and whether they are speeding up or slowing down. These last two senses are particularly important to flying insects.

This grasshopper, from southern Africa, has ears on either side of its abdomen. Each ear consists of an oval drum that lies level with the insect's body. Sounds make the drum vibrate, and this sends signals to the grasshopper's brain. Many crickets have ears on their legs.

Cockroaches escape their enemies by running, and they sense danger by using special bristles that detect vibrations in the ground. When anything approaches, this causes vibrations. The cockroach senses them, and within a fraction of a second it is dashing for cover.

FEEDING AND DIGESTION

Unlike us, insects do not have jaws and teeth. Instead, their mouths are surrounded by special mouthparts. In the four insects shown here, the mouthparts form a tube or a spongy pad. These insects eat liquid food, and use their mouthparts to suck up a meal.

BUTTERFLIES AND MOSQUITOES

Butterflies drink sugary nectar from flowers. In order to reach the nectar, they have very long, tube-like mouthparts, called a proboscis. When not in use, the proboscis conveniently rolls up.

Mosquitoes have sharp mouthparts that work together like a syringe. A mosquito pushes them into skin, and then sucks up a meal of blood. Only female mosquitoes feed on blood. Males live mainly on nectar collected from flowers.

A butterfly's long proboscis reaches into a flower for nectar. As the butterfly feeds, its crop fills up with nectar which is then gradually released to the stomach.

When a female mosquito feeds on blood, its crop swells up and the under-side of its abdomen turns dark red. The females need a blood meal before they can lay their eggs.

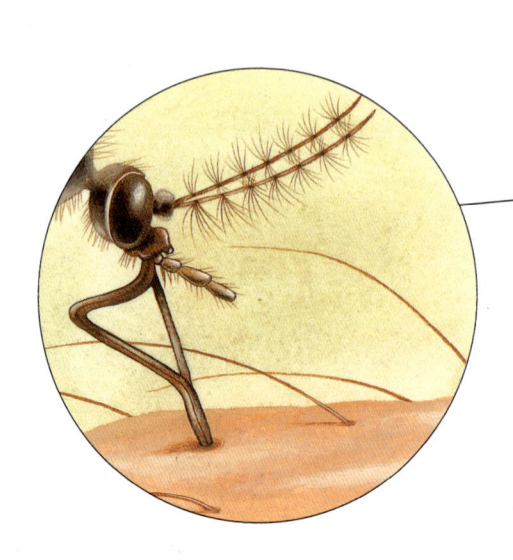

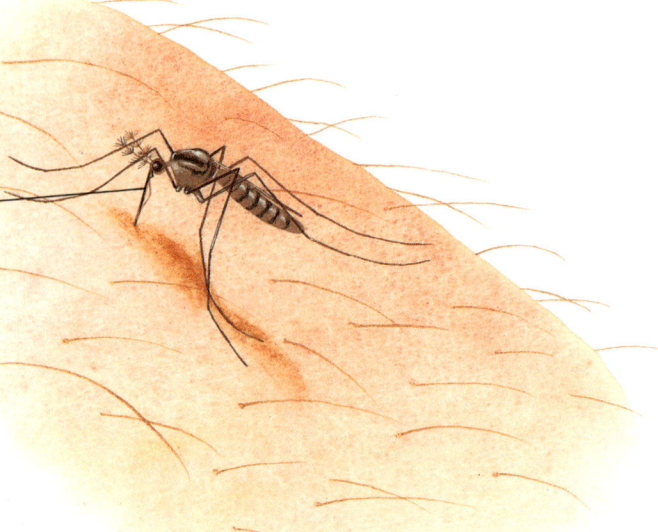

HOUSEFLIES AND APHIDS

A housefly's mouthparts end in a sponge-like pad called a haustellum. The fly feeds by pouring saliva on to the surface of the pad. The saliva then dissolves the fly's food, and the fly sucks up the nutritious fluid. Flies often leave small sticky spots that show where they have been feeding.

An aphid has a small needle-like beak called a rostrum. It pushes this into a plant's stem or leaves, and feeds on its sugary sap. The sap inside plants is under pressure, so it squirts into the aphid's body without having to be sucked up.

DIGESTIVE SYSTEMS

Like ours, an insect's digestive system is based around a tube that runs through its body. The tube is normally divided into several chambers. The first of these is usually the crop. This has stretchy walls, and it stores food when the insect is eating, and then gradually releases it so that it can be digested.

Insects that eat solid food, such as grasshoppers and some beetles, also have a chamber called the gizzard. This helps break up food. The mid-gut or stomach absorbs digested food into the body, and undigested material is passed out.

Houseflies make lots of saliva to dissolve their food. This is produced by glands in the fly's head. When a housefly has a large meal, its crop swells up with liquid food. This is slowly released so it can be digested.

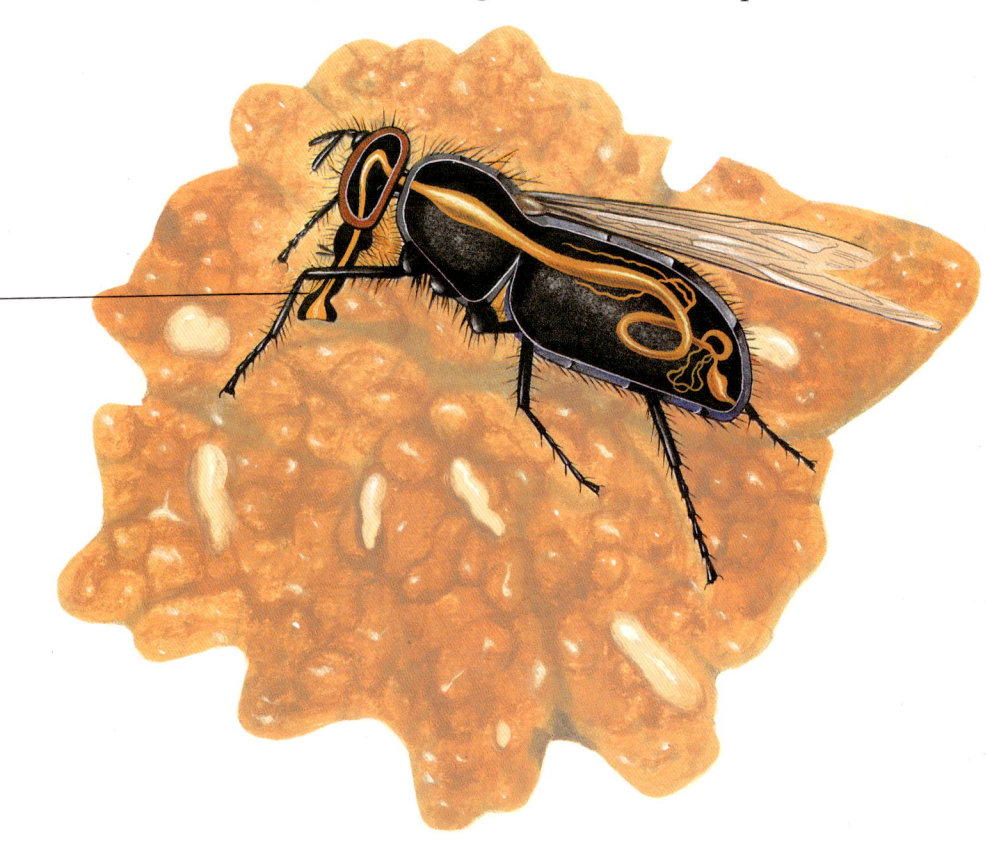

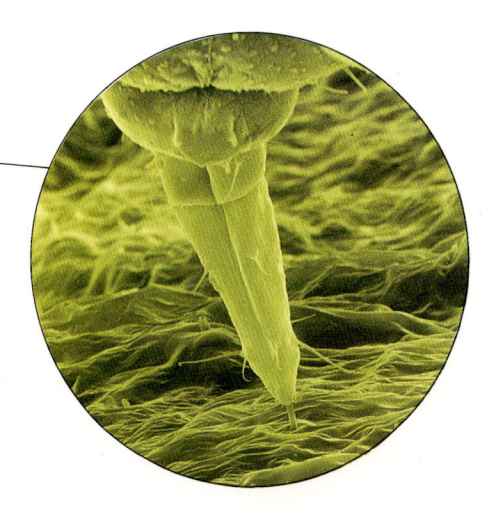

Aphids feed on sap, which is a very watery fluid that contains dissolved sugar. The aphid therefore has to get rid of a lot of watery waste. It stores this in a chamber called the rectum before squeezing it out of its body.

KEEPING IN TOUCH

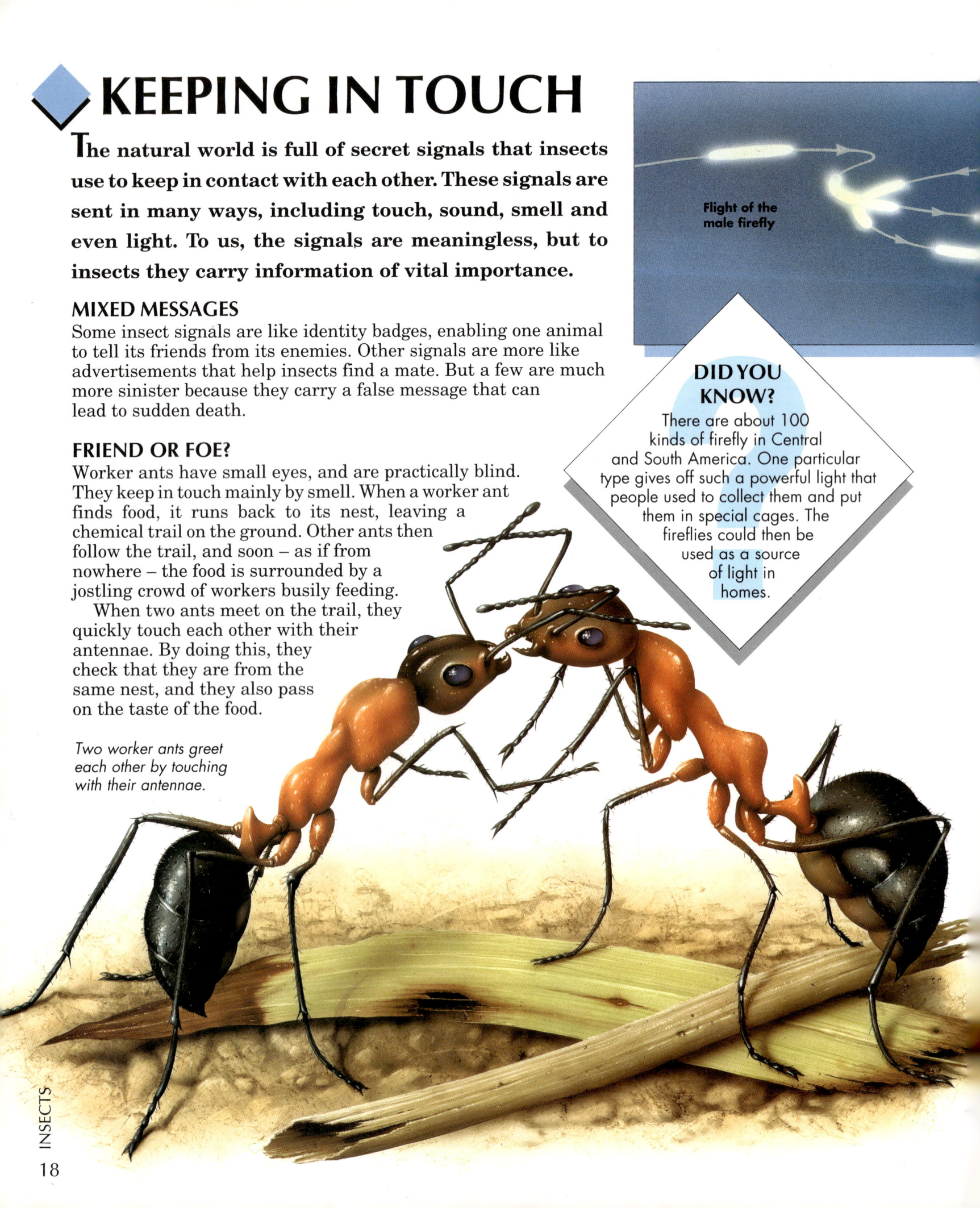

The natural world is full of secret signals that insects use to keep in contact with each other. These signals are sent in many ways, including touch, sound, smell and even light. To us, the signals are meaningless, but to insects they carry information of vital importance.

Flight of the male firefly

MIXED MESSAGES

Some insect signals are like identity badges, enabling one animal to tell its friends from its enemies. Other signals are more like advertisements that help insects find a mate. But a few are much more sinister because they carry a false message that can lead to sudden death.

FRIEND OR FOE?

Worker ants have small eyes, and are practically blind. They keep in touch mainly by smell. When a worker ant finds food, it runs back to its nest, leaving a chemical trail on the ground. Other ants then follow the trail, and soon – as if from nowhere – the food is surrounded by a jostling crowd of workers busily feeding.

When two ants meet on the trail, they quickly touch each other with their antennae. By doing this, they check that they are from the same nest, and they also pass on the taste of the food.

Two worker ants greet each other by touching with their antennae.

DID YOU KNOW?

There are about 100 kinds of firefly in Central and South America. One particular type gives off such a powerful light that people used to collect them and put them in special cages. The fireflies could then be used as a source of light in homes.

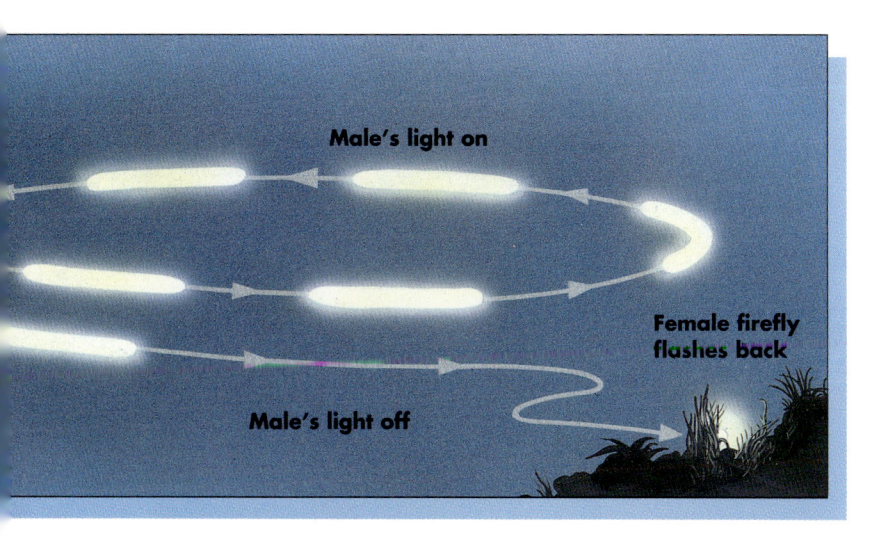

MAKING SOUND

In many parts of the world, warm weather brings a chorus of insect calls. During the day, the sound is made mainly by grasshoppers and crickets. At night, it is made by large plant-sucking bugs called cicadas.

If you creep up on a grasshopper, you may be lucky enough to see how it makes its call.

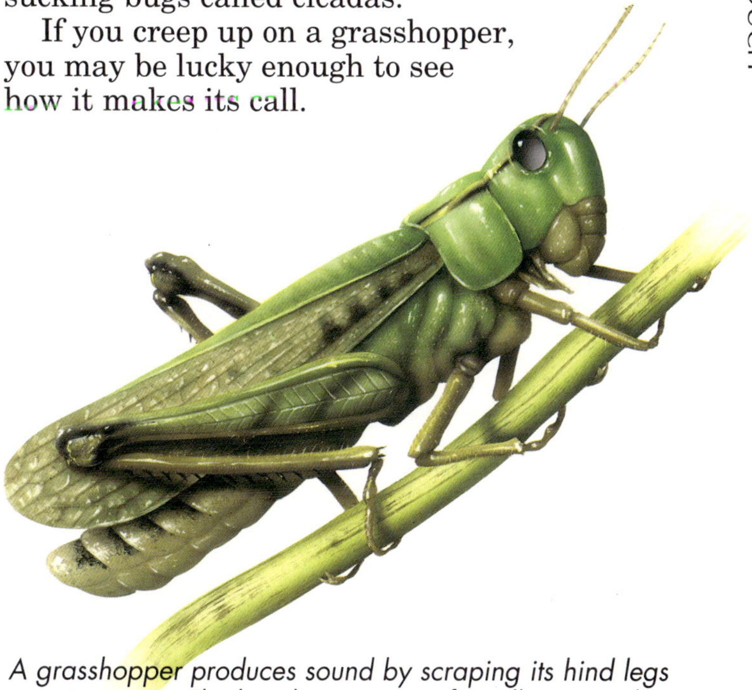

Fireflies are small beetles that live in warm parts of the world. Males and females communicate by short coded flashes of light. However, the code is not always foolproof. Some female fireflies imitate the code of other species, and when a male approaches the light, the female grabs him. Instead of mating with him, she eats him.

UNDERGROUND BROADCAST

The mole cricket spends nearly all its life underground. During the breeding season, males use sound to get in touch with females. They rub their wings together, and this makes a whirring call that can be heard hundreds of metres away. One species of mole cricket digs a specially shaped burrow with two funnel-like entrances. The burrow works like an amplifier, so that the cricket's call is broadcast far and wide.

A grasshopper produces sound by scraping its hind legs over its wings. The legs have a row of small pegs in the inner surface, and these make its wings vibrate. This way of making sound is called stridulation.

Glow-worms are not real worms, but small beetles. Here, two wingless female glow-worms give off a greenish light to attract males. They make the light on the underside of their abdomens, and twist them upwards so the light is visible from above. Winged males flying nearby see the light, and come down to mate.

HOW INSECTS REPRODUCE

Almost all insects start life as eggs. Insect eggs are so small that we rarely notice them, but they are tough, and can survive freezing cold and scorching heat. Before egg-laying can start, the female usually has to mate.

FLYING TOGETHER
Damselflies grow up in water, and the female lays her eggs inside underwater plants. During mating, the male clasps the female by her neck, and the pair then fly off over a pond or stream, with their bodies locked together. From time to time, the female settles on a plant and inches her abdomen beneath the water surface. The tip of her abdomen slices open a plant, and she lays a single egg inside. This kind of pairing up is quite unusual in the insect world, because most female insects lay eggs on their own.

A female damselfly lays eggs while flying in tandem with her mate. The female may dip her abdomen in the water, or submerge herself entirely.

Not all insects have to mate before producing young. This unmated female aphid is giving birth to a baby, and she is surrounded by her growing single-parent family. During late spring and early summer, unmated female aphids can produce several babies a day.

DID YOU KNOW?
In the Arctic, scientists have found that aphid eggs can survive temperatures below -25°C (-13°F). This is much colder than a household deep-freeze.

COURTSHIP GIFTS

For male insects, mating can be a dangerous activity. Females are often larger than their partners, and will sometimes kill and eat them.

Male dance flies have evolved an interesting way to get around this problem. During courtship, the male presents the female with the gift of a dead insect. While she is absorbed in eating her 'present', the male can safely mate with her.

Most insects abandon their eggs when they have laid them. However, a few species, including this green plant bug, look after their eggs and protect their young until they are ready to fend for themselves. These careful parents usually lay fewer eggs than other insects, but they give their young a better chance of survival.

Two mating dance flies hang from a leaf. The male, on the far left, holds on with his legs, while the female eats a leafhopper that he has presented to her. Male dance flies often wrap up the female's 'gift' in a cocoon of silk. Sometimes they cheat, and the female opens the cocoon only to find that it is empty.

AMAZING EGGS

Most insect eggs are smaller than a pinhead and have a tough outer shell. Some insects drop their eggs from the air, but many carefully fasten them to plants so that their young will hatch close to food.

Some insect eggs hatch soon after they are laid, while others stay dormant for months. This long interval allows some species to survive through difficult times of the year, when all the adults die.

Stick insects drop their eggs on the ground. Each one has a lid that pops open when the egg hatches.

Some lacewings lay their eggs on stalks so they are out of the reach of other animals.

The large white butterfly lays its bright yellow eggs in clusters on cabbage plants.

Cockroaches lay eggs in a small package. The mother carries it until the eggs hatch.

CHANGING SHAPE

In order to grow, an insect has to shed its skin, or moult. For a while, the new skin is soft and so the insect's body can expand. However, each time the insect sheds its skin it does not just get bigger, it can also change shape. This is called metamorphosis. In some insects, metamorphosis happens gradually, and in others it happens suddenly, and the insect's body is completely altered.

WHY CHANGE SHAPE?

Insects change shape so they can make the most of different foods, and so they can spread. For example, a caterpillar has powerful jaws and lives on leaves, but a butterfly has a long tongue and lives on sugary nectar. Caterpillars cannot travel far, but butterflies can fly a long way, and this enables the species to reach new sources of food.

A SUDDEN CHANGE

A caterpillar is an example of a 'larva'. A larva looks completely different from its parents, and usually eats different food.

Caterpillars moult several times. They get bigger after each moult, but their shape usually stays the same. Then something dramatic happens. The caterpillar stops eating, and turns into a chrysalis. During this resting stage, its body is broken down and completely rearranged to make a butterfly. When this process is complete, the adult butterfly emerges.

This kind of development is called complete metamorphosis. It is found in many other insects, including beetles, flies, wasps, bees and ants.

Silk moth caterpillars turn into adults inside cocoons made of silk. The cocoons can be unwound and the silk used for clothes.

The adult butterfly breaks out of the chrysalis, and its wings spread out. It is now ready to breed.

The swallowtail butterfly lays its eggs singly, and fastens them on to the caterpillar's food plants.

The swallowtail caterpillar feeds for several weeks. It has three pairs of legs and several sucker-like prolegs.

The caterpillar eventually stops feeding, and forms a chrysalis or pupa. Inside the chrysalis, most of the caterpillar's body dissolves. A new body then takes shape.

Some dragonflies lay their eggs on or inside water plants. Others scatter them over the surface of ponds and slow-moving streams.

A dragonfly nymph hunts small animals using a set of hinged mouthparts called a mask (see page 29). Like the adult, it has six legs, but its wings are just small buds.

When the nymph is fully grown, it climbs up a plant stem and out of the water. Its skin splits open, and an adult dragonfly slowly climbs out. The adult waits for its wings to expand and harden before flying off.

Some insects moult just two or three times in their lives, while others moult 25 times or more. Winged insects usually stop moulting once they have become adult, and they do not grow any more. Simple wingless insects, such as silverfish, moult throughout their lives, and may keep getting bigger.

A GRADUAL CHANGE

A young dragonfly is called a 'nymph'. A nymph looks quite like its parents, but it does not have working wings or reproductive organs. Dragonfly nymphs live underwater, and they moult about a dozen times. Each time a dragonfly nymph moults, its eyes get bigger, and so do its wing buds. Eventually, the nymph climbs out of the water and sheds its skin for the last time. Its wings spread out and harden, and the adult dragonfly takes off and flies away.

This way of developing is called incomplete or partial metamorphosis, because the insect's body changes only slightly as it grows up. Grasshoppers, cockroaches and true bugs also grow up in this way.

Dragonflies grow up underwater, but they spend their adult lives in the air. Instead of using their mouthparts to catch prey, adult dragonflies use their legs. They have very keen eyesight so they can grab flying insects in mid-air.

CHANGING SHAPE

INSECT ARCHITECTS

Using simple raw materials, and guided entirely by instinct, some insects build amazing structures. Here, you can find out about two of the most elaborate buildings in the insect world – the paper nests of wasps, and the mud nests of termites.

HOW A WASP NEST IS BUILT

Common wasps build their nests from paper, which they make by chewing up fibres of wood. The finished nest is like a multi-storey building, with several floors connected by pillars.

1 The queen selects a solid support, such as a wooden beam. She starts the nest by making a paper cup with a thread hanging from its centre.

2 The queen then builds a small cluster of cells, and extends the cup to make a case. She lays eggs in the cells.

3 The first batch of eggs hatch, producing worker wasps. These take over the building work. They extend the nest, tearing down the old case and building new layers of cells.

4 As more worker wasps hatch and develop, the nest expands rapidly. Within four months, it can be as big as a football and may contain over 10,000 cells.

OUTSIDE A TERMITE NEST

Termites are the master builders of the insect world. Their nests have many shapes and sizes. Some look like mushrooms or footballs, while others are like towers or flat-sided slabs. Termites that nest in trees often make their nests from wood fibres, but ones that nest in the ground make their nests from mud.

The giant nests shown here are built by a species of termite called *Macrotermes*, which lives in Africa. Its nests are made of mud, and can be over 6 metres high. When the mud is freshly mixed, it is quite soft and easy for the termites to use. But once the Sun has baked it dry, it turns almost as hard as rock.

INSIDE THE NEST

A *Macrotermes* nest consists of two different parts. Near ground level is a large, round dome containing lots of small chambers. Some of these chambers contain special 'gardens', which the termites use to grow a fungus that they eat. One large chamber contains the queen termite, while others house eggs that are waiting to hatch. Above the dome is a spire. This is the nest's air conditioning system. Its wide ventilation ducts allow air to circulate through the nest.

TUNNELS INSIDE
1. Spire of sunbaked mud
2. Ventilation duct
3. Fungus garden
4. Chamber for queen termite
5. Nursery areas

INSECT ARCHITECTS

INCREDIBLE JOURNEYS

Despite their small size, insects are often well-travelled animals. The butterflies you see in a garden may have grown up hundreds of miles away, and will often move on as soon as they have fed. These long-distance journeys are called migrations. Insects migrate in step with the seasons, to make the best use of food in summer, and to escape the cold in winter.

In autumn, huge numbers of monarch butterflies make their way to the highlands of central Mexico. They roost on trees, completely covering them as they crowd together.

BUTTERFLIES ON THE MOVE

Butterflies are the champion migrants of the insect world. Although their flight looks weak and fluttery, they can move at a steady 10 kilometres an hour for many hours a day. If the wind is light, they fly at about rooftop height, but if it is strong, they keep much closer to the ground.

Butterflies navigate by the Sun. Many of them stay at a constant angle to the Sun, and this makes them follow a curved path as the Sun moves across the sky.

AIRBORNE INVADERS

Locusts are grasshoppers that live in dry parts of the world. Normally, they search for food on their own. But if food becomes scarce and the locusts are crowded, their behaviour completely changes. The locusts band together to form immense swarms, and they fly off in search of food.

A locust swarm can cover 1,000 square kilometres, and may contain several billion insects. When the swarm settles, the locusts devastate crops and other plants. Locusts are found in Africa, the Americas and Australia.

Monarch butterflies can journey up to 3,200 kilometres as they fly from cold northerly regions to the warmer south for winter.

These young locusts or 'hoppers' cannot fly, and they must move across the ground in search of food. Once they have fully-grown wings, the locust swarm will take to the air.

INCREDIBLE JOURNEYS

Painted lady butterflies live all over the world. The ones that hatch out in North Africa migrate across Europe, and often reach as far as Scandinavia, a distance of 2,900 kilometres. In warm years, they can even cross the Arctic Circle.

Most ants build permanent nests, and spend their lives in one area. Army ants and driver ants are different. For much of their lives, these fearsome tropical ants form marauding columns that sweep across the ground, killing and eating any animals in their path. A single 'army' contains millions of ants, and can cover about 500 metres a day.

Processionary moth caterpillars get their name because they move about in single file. If a few of them are put on the rim of a cup, they follow each other around in endless circles.

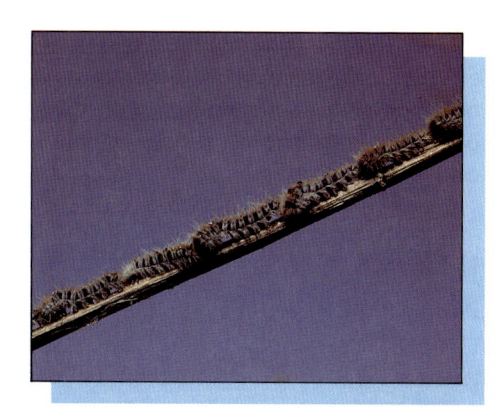

INVISIBLE TRAVELLERS

During spring and summer the air is full of tiny insects that are blown about by the wind. These midget migrants are not strong enough to follow a set path. Instead, they use the wind like a conveyor belt. They jump on at one place, and are carried along in the air, until they settle somewhere, often far away.

Thrips, or thunderbugs, often live in flowers. They take to the air in hot, thundery weather and can be carried far away during storms.

In summer, wingless aphids produce winged young. The young aphids form huge swarms that are blown high into the air.

Booklice live in dry places and under bark, as well as in books. Winged booklice look like aphids, and they travel in the same way.

35

CAMOUFLAGE AND MIMICRY

For many insects, the best way to escape attack is to look like something that is not worth attacking. Some insects use camouflage to blend in with their background, so they are almost impossible to see. Others mimic inedible things such as a twig or a thorn. Or they might pretend to be dangerous.

NOW YOU SEE THEM...

On these two pages, you can see over a dozen different insects. They are easy to spot because they stand out against their background. All of them have a conspicuous outline and some have very bright colours.

If they were as visible as this in real life, they would not survive for long. They would soon be spotted by sharp-eyed birds and mammals, and would make an easy meal. But the colours and shapes you can see here are not such a give-away as they seem.

If you now turn over the see-through page, you will find out what the insects actually look like in their natural habitat, where they use camouflage or mimicry to disguise themselves.

... AND NOW YOU DON'T

Here the insects are surrounded by plants, and are far harder to see. Some of them have colours and patterns that look just like bark, flowers, or moss. This camouflage is so effective that they are almost impossible to pick out from their background. Others, such as the stick insects and katydids, mimic parts of plants. And one caterpillar even imitates a bird's droppings!

Most butterflies hide away by closing up their brightly-coloured wings. But if they are threatened, some – including the owl butterfly (1) – reveal brightly coloured eyespots that deter potential predators. The hawkmoth caterpillar (7) reacts to danger by rearing up and swaying from side to side like a miniature snake.

HIDDEN INSECTS

1. Owl butterfly
2. Green stick insect
3. Brown stick insect
4. Spotted-leaf katydid
5. Pink flower mantid
6. Green spiny caterpillar
7. Hawkmoth caterpillar
8. Leaf butterfly
9. Bushcricket
10. Hawkmoth caterpillar
11. Green katydid
12. Marbled beauty moth
13. Green brindled beauty moth
14. Thornbugs

INSECT COLOURS

What do you think insects and cars have in common? The answer is that they come in all the colours of the rainbow, and in a variety of finishes. But unlike cars, insects get their spectacular colours in two quite different ways. Some insect colours are produced by chemicals called pigments, which work like the chemicals in paints. Others are created by microscopic structures on the surface of the insect's body.

Leaf beetles often look like drops of liquid gold or silver. Their colours are produced by a layered body case.

BEAUTY ON THE WING

Morphos are some of the world's most beautiful butterflies. In bright sunlight, the males have a brilliant metallic blue colour, but in dull light they often look brown. Morphos produce their colour by reflecting light in a special way. Their wings are covered with tiny scales that have upright flaps. When sunlight strikes the flaps, most of it is absorbed, but the blue part of the light is reflected and strengthened through a process called interference. This is the secret of the morpho's jewel-like sheen. Interference colours do not fade when an insect dies, which is why morphos are sought after by butterfly collectors.

METALLIC COLOURS

Many insects make shiny or 'iridescent' colours by interfering with waves of light. Some use special scales like the morpho butterfly, but others use microscopic hairs, or thin layers of body casing separated by air-filled spaces. Their colours often seem to alter as the animal's position changes.

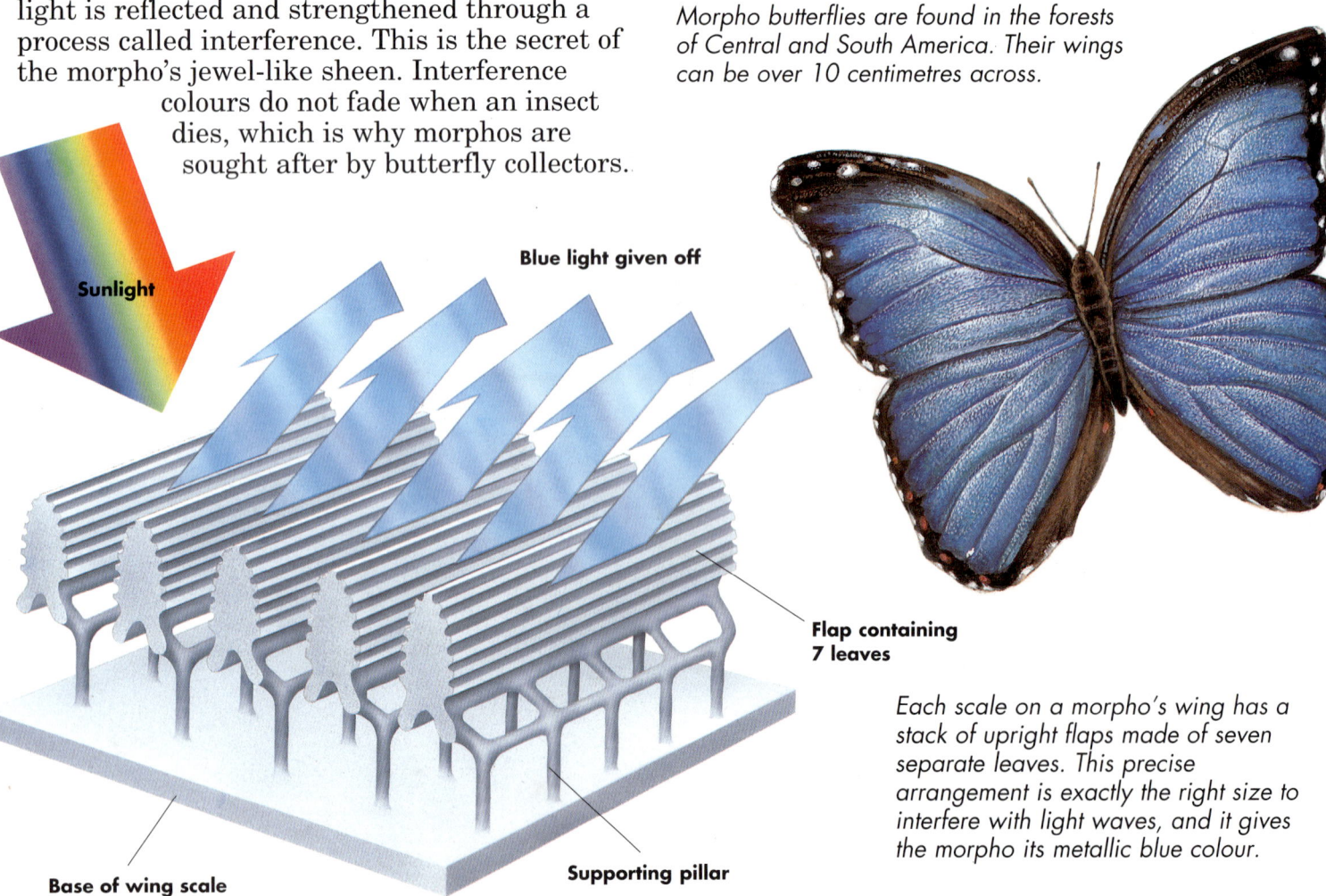

Morpho butterflies are found in the forests of Central and South America. Their wings can be over 10 centimetres across.

Sunlight

Blue light given off

Flap containing 7 leaves

Base of wing scale

Supporting pillar

Each scale on a morpho's wing has a stack of upright flaps made of seven separate leaves. This precise arrangement is exactly the right size to interfere with light waves, and it gives the morpho its metallic blue colour.

INSECTS

42

WARNING COLOURS

Some insects use colours to make themselves conspicuous. By doing this, they show that they have a secret weapon which makes them dangerous to attack. Usually this weapon is some kind of poison that is either stored in the insect's body, or is injected through a sting.

The ladybird is brightly coloured and its body tastes unpleasant.

The cinnabar moth's strong colours warn that its body is poisonous.

Hornets and wasps are easily seen and are avoided because of their stings.

Many weevils have bright colours. These are produced by microscopic hairs, and by the structure of the weevil's body case.

Many damselflies and dragonflies are coloured blue by tiny granules on the surface of their bodies. These granules scatter blue light, so that is the colour we see.

COLOURS FROM CHEMICALS

The clouded yellow butterfly gets its colour by storing chemicals in its wings. The chemicals are waste products left over after the butterfly has digested its food. Many other butterflies make orange or red colours in the same way. These chemical colours look the same from whatever angle you view them.

PAINTED BLACK

Many insects are black. Black is not really a colour – it is simply what you see when something absorbs all the light that falls on it. Black insects absorb light with a chemical called melanin. The same chemical makes human hair black, and turns skin turn dark when it is exposed to sunshine.

The devil's coach-horse is a sinister-looking beetle that hunts on the ground. It is completely black.

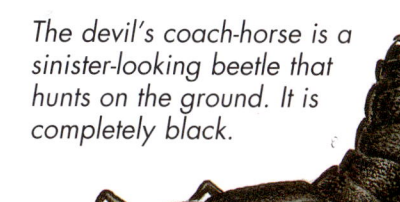

Unlike metallic colours, chemical colours such as those of the clouded yellow butterfly often fade after the butterfly has died.

43

INSECTS INDOORS

Our homes have two things that we all enjoy – warmth and food. Unfortunately, insects also like being warm and well fed, which is why many find their way indoors. Some of these uninvited lodgers eat the same things that we do, but others feast on things we would find distinctly unappetizing, such as wood, glue, clothes and carpets.

INSIDE A KITCHEN

1 Silverfish are small wingless insects that feed on starchy food such as breadcrumbs and dry wallpaper paste. They are nocturnal, and scuttle away when disturbed. They rarely build up to large numbers.

2 Booklice are some of the smallest insects that live in houses. They live on moulds that grow in damp places, and can be found in old books, on moist wood and plaster, and in damp starchy food such as old flour.

3 Clothes moths are one of the most serious insect pests indoors. As caterpillars, they feed on anything that contains wool, and not just clothes. The adult moth is small and golden, and has a dusty texture.

4 House-flies are temporary visitors to houses. They buzz about in search of food, and lay their eggs in rubbish and rotting waste.

5 Cockroaches are probably the most hated of all indoor insects. They feed at night on many kinds of food, from bread to soap, and give anything they touch an unpleasant smell.

6 House crickets are relatives of grasshoppers. They live on all kinds of leftovers, but rarely do much harm. They come from warm parts of the world, but survive in cold places inside heated houses.

CONTROLLING INSECTS

At one time, people had very few ways of keeping insects out of their homes. Today, we use many different methods to keep these unwelcome visitors at bay.

Moth balls contain a chemical that spreads through cupboards, killing clothes moths.

Fly-strips are coated with glue. When flies land on them, they soon become stuck fast.

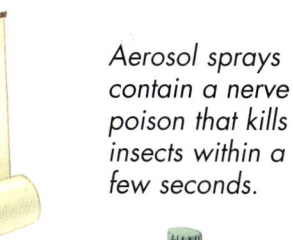

Aerosol sprays contain a nerve poison that kills insects within a few seconds.

Electric fly-killers attract flying insects by giving off ultraviolet light. The insects fly into a metal grid and are electrocuted.

Screens over doors and windows stop flying insects from getting into houses.

FEEDING ON WOOD

For humans, wood is a useful building material, but for some insects, it is an abundant source of food. There are two main groups of wood-eating insects – beetles and termites. Beetle grubs often live inside wood, boring tunnels as they feed. Termites usually chew away wood in small pieces, and take it back to their nests. Given enough time, these insects can weaken timber so much that it collapses.

A woodworm is not a true worm, but the grub of the common furniture beetle. It bores its way through furniture and timbers, and leaves small circular holes where it emerges as an adult beetle, shown above. Woodworm can spread from one house to another when people move, bringing infested furniture with them.

INDEX

abdomen 4, 5, 6, 8-9, 10, 39
air-tubes 10, 11
antennae 6, 8, 14, 15
ant-lion larvae 38
ants 14, 18, 30-31, 39
    army 35
    driver 30, 35
    honeypot 31
    leafcutter 30-31
    slavemaker 30
aphids 17, 20, 35

backswimmer 11, 29
bees 5, 12, 26, 30-31, 39
    green 27
    honey 7, 14, 44
beetles 5, 6, 12
    bombardier 39
    goliath 7
    great diving 28
    leaf 42
    stag 38
    tiger 14
    woodworm 47
blood system 8-9
bloodworms 29
bluebottles 24
body case 4, 6-7, 42-43
booklice 35, 46
brain 9, 14, 15
breathing 10-11, 28-29
bugs 5, 21, 28, 29
butterflies 5, 7, 13, 15, 16
    clouded yellow 43
    large white 21, 37
    monarch 34
    morpho 42
    owl 41
    painted lady 35
    red admiral 14
    swallowtail 22, 39
    tortoiseshell 24

camouflage 39, 40-41
caterpillars 6, 11
    hawkmoth 41
    large blue 37
    processionary moth 35
    tortoiseshell 24
    swallowtail 22, 39
    vapourer moth 39
chrysalis 22, 24
cicadas 7, 19, 25
cockchafer 15
cockroaches 15, 21, 25, 46
colours 40-41, 42-43
communication 18-19
cranefly 12
crickets 10, 19, 46
    bush- 10, 15, 41

damselflies 4, 20, 43
devil's coach horse 43
digestive system 4, 17
diseases 44-45
dragonflies 5, 14, 23, 43
    nymph 29

ears 15
eggs 9, 20-21, 22-23, 24-25
elytra 6, 12
eyes 4, 9, 14
eyespots 41

fireflies 18-19
fleas 10, 36
flies 5, 12, 13
    braconid 37
    dance 21
    house- 17, 45, 46
flight 12-13

galls 26
gills 11, 29
glow-worms 19
grasshoppers 5, 8-9, 10, 15, 19

halteres 12
haustellum 17
hibernation 25
hornets 43

ichneumons 37

katydids 41

lacewings 13, 21
ladybird 12, 43
larvae 11, 22, 24, 28-29, 36
lice 36
life cycles 24-25
locusts 34

maggots 11, 24
mantis 41
    praying 38
mating 9, 20-21, 24, 30
mayflies 11, 25
melanin 43
metamorphosis 22-23
midges 27, 29
migration 34-35
mimicry 40-41
mosquitoes 11, 13, 16, 28, 44-45
moths 13, 14, 41
    atlas 7
    cinnabar 43
    clothes 46
    green brindled beauty 41
    marbled beauty 41
    processionary 35

silk 22
Urania 7
vapourer 39
yucca 27
moulting 7, 11, 22-23
mouthparts 4, 16-17, 23, 29
muscles 6, 8-9, 13

nests 32-33
nymphs 23, 25, 29

ocelli 14
oxygen 10-11, 29

parasites 36-37
pigments 42
poisons 38-39, 43
pollination 26-27
pondskaters 28
proboscis 16
pupa 22, 24

reproduction 20-21
reproductive organs 4, 9

sawflies 26
scales 5, 7, 13, 42
segments 5, 6
senses 4, 9, 14-15
silverfish 23, 46
social insects 30-31
spiracles 10, 11
springtails 5
stick insects 21, 41
stings 39
stridulation 19
swarms 31, 34, 44

termites 24, 30-31, 32, 47
thorax 4, 6, 13
thornbugs 41
thrips 13, 35
thunderbugs 13, 35
tsetse fly 45

underwater insects 11, 23, 25, 28-29

wasps 5, 12, 13, 30-31, 39, 43
    chalcid 24
    common 32
    fig 27
    gall 26
    parasitic 37
    queen 25, 32
water-scorpion 29
weapons 38-39
weevil 15, 43
wings 4-5, 8, 12-13, 42
woodlice 4
woodworm 47